MATTER
AND
MATERIALS

Peter Mellett

KINGFISHER

This edition published 2013 by Kingfisher
an imprint of Macmillan Children's Books
a division of Macmillan Publishers Limited
20 New Wharf Road, London N1 9RR
Basingstoke and Oxford
Associated companies throughout the world
www.panmacmillan.com

Created for Kingfisher by The Book Makers Ltd
Illustrations: Peter Bull Art Studio

ISBN 978-0-7534-3370-6

Copyright © Macmillan Children's Books 2013

10 9 8 7 6 5 4 3 2 1
1TR/1212/UG/WKT/140MA

A CIP catalogue record for this book is available from the British Library.

Printed in China

Note to readers:
The website addresses listed in this book are correct at the time
of going to print. However, due to the ever-changing nature of
the internet, website addresses and content can change. Websites
can contain links that are unsuitable for
children. The publisher cannot be held
responsible for changes in website
addresses or content, or for information
obtained through a third party. We
strongly advise that internet searches
be supervised by an adult.

Cover credits: tl Alamy/Janine Weidel;
tc Shutterstock/BestPhotoByMonikaGniot;
tr Shutterstock/matka_Waratka; bl Shutterstock/
Tatiana Gladskikh; br Shutterstock/
Dmitriy Shironosov

Salt

Sugar

Soda

Contents

Getting started

The world we live in is made from matter, but what exactly is this? Matter includes anything that has mass and takes up space. Our bodies, the air we breathe and the water we drink are all examples of matter. The different types of matter that we use to make things from are called materials.

Stuck for words?

If you come across a word you don't understand, or you just want to find out a bit more, have a look in the glossary on pages 30 and 31.

Clock symbol

The clock symbol in each experiment shows you how many minutes the activity should take. All take between 5 and 30 minutes. If you are using glue, allow extra time for drying.

Some materials, such as rocks, soil, water and wood, are natural. Other materials are manufactured by people, such as metals, glass and paper.

All matter and materials behave differently. This book will show you how materials are tested and chosen before they are used in manufacturing or building.

The right stuff

You'll need a few everyday things such as string, rubber bands, a plastic bottle and some other items you can find in the kitchen.

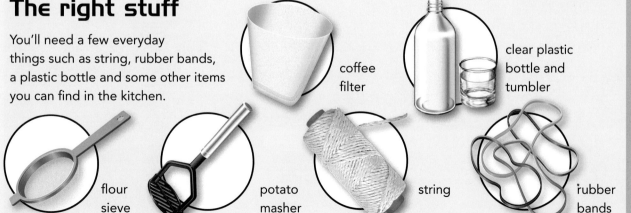

coffee filter

clear plastic bottle and tumbler

flour sieve

potato masher

string

rubber bands

Warning

Some activities involve heat or flames, or the use of a hammer. Ask an adult for help with these, and with any other activities where you see this warning symbol, or if you think an activity may be difficult to do alone.

Don't touch your face or rub your eyes, especially if you are using materials such as salt, washing soda or soil. Try not to get glue on your hands.

Always wash your hands and scrub your nails thoroughly after you have finished working. It is important to remove some substances immediately.

Getting organized

Carry out your experiments on a firm table. Don't forget to cover it first with old newspaper, to protect its surface from spills, dirt and mess.

If you need to pour water, put a shallow tray underneath to catch any spills and overflow.

When using a hammer, first put down an old chopping board, or another piece of wood, on a firm surface like a table, or directly onto the floor.

Having problems?

☹ Don't give up if at first you have problems with some of the activities. Even Einstein had his bad days!

☺ If things don't seem to be working, read through each step of the activity again and then have another go.

If you get stuck, an adult at home, or a teacher at school, may be able to explain things to you.

Soil mixture

Soil is one of the most important materials in the world. Nearly all plants need soil to grow and most animals depend on plants as the source of their food. If there was no soil, there would be almost no life on the land. There are many different sorts of soil, but all of them are a mixture of sand, clay and humus, the rotted remains of dead plants.

What's going on?

Water drains through soil by trickling through the spaces between the particles. Not all the added water drains out because some is absorbed by the clay and humus in the soil. The sandier the soil, the more water will drain out, because sand does not absorb water. Clay particles are hundreds of times smaller than sand grains. They block the spaces between sand and humus and slow the downward movement of water. Water cannot pass at all through some clay soils.

Testing soil

Find out what your local soil is like. How much water does it absorb and how well does water drain through it?

You will need:

- Dry soil
- A 500ml plastic drinks bottle
- A spoon
- Scissors
- Cotton wool
- A tablespoon
- A measuring jug of water

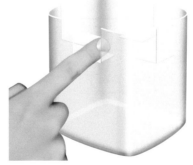

I Cut the bottle in half. Make two cuts down each side of the lower part of the bottle. Fold the cut parts inwards to make four tabs.

2 Turn the top half of the bottle upside down to make a funnel. Now push it down into the bottom half so that the cut tabs grip the bottle neck. Push a ball of cotton wool into the bottle neck.

What's in your soil?

Quarter fill the bottle with soil and then fill two thirds of it with water. Screw on the cap and shake hard. Let the bottle stand and watch the different layers form as the soil settles.

You will need:

- A plastic bottle with a cap
- Dry soil
- Water

What's going on?

Large grains of sand and gravel are the first to settle to the bottom. The next layer up is fine, silty sand, followed by clay particles. Floating above the clay layer are tiny clay particles too small to settle to the bottom. You may also see humus floating on the surface. By testing different soil samples, you can see how soil varies from place to place.

3 Add six tablespoons of soil and then gently pour in 200ml of water. Time how long it takes the water to pass through the soil. Then measure the amount of water that runs out of the soil.

Stretching and snapping

The extent to which a material can be pulled and stretched is called its tensile strength. Engineers choose materials with great tensile strength to do certain jobs. The high-tensile steel cable of a crane is able to support a very heavy load.

Threads and wires

Compare the tensile strength of three different materials. Remember to repeat the activity using a different thread each time!

You will need:

- A 2-litre plastic bottle
- A broom handle
- Two kitchen stools or chairs
- A measuring jug containing a litre of water
- A marker pen
- Three threads of the same thickness, e.g. wool, dental floss (nylon), fuse wire (copper)

1 Lie the broom flat on top of the two stools, as shown in the picture above.

2 Slowly, pour a litre of water into the bottle. Mark the water level on the bottle for every 100ml you pour. 100ml of water has a mass of 100g, so label the marks 100g, 200g, 300g and so on.

3 Tip the water out. Tie the end of one thread around the neck of the bottle and the other end around the broom handle. The bottle should hang a little above the floor.

Testing thin sheets

Cut out strips of each material 1cm wide by 15cm long. Wrap a strip tightly around the clothes peg and hold it firmly. Squeeze the peg harder and harder until the material breaks. Do this with each strip.

You will need:

- Thin sheets of material, e.g. clingfilm, a crisp packet, a paper towel and newspaper
- A clothes peg
- Scissors

What's going on?

Some materials are more elastic than others, so they stretch further before they break. Paper materials are made from particles called fibres, which break apart easily. Plastic materials such as clingfilm are made from particles called molecules. These hold strongly together, stretching before they part.

What's going on?

Gravity pulls downwards on the water in the bottle. This creates a pulling force called tension in the thread, which causes it to stretch and then snap. How quickly it snaps depends on how thick the thread is and what it is made from. Wool, a natural fibre, isn't very strong. Dental floss, made from a plastic called nylon, and copper wire both have a much greater tensile strength than wool.

4 Support the bottle with one hand and slowly pour in the water. After every 100ml, replace the cap, then let your hand go. When the thread breaks, note the water level in the bottle. Repeat steps 3 and 4 with the other threads. Which one lasts the longest without breaking?

9

Moving heat

Heat moves through solids by a process called conduction. Some materials, such as metals, allow heat to pass easily. They are good conductors of heat. Other materials, such as paper and plastics, do not allow heat to pass easily. They are called insulators and are poor conductors of heat. We use insulating materials to keep things warm.

What's going on?

The water in the mug sealed inside the polythene bag should stay the hottest, while the water in the uncovered mug is the coolest. Air is a good insulator, so long as it doesn't move around too much. The polythene bag holds a layer of air around the mug that stops heat escaping. Cotton wool contains air trapped in its fibres. Newspaper also contains air, but less than cotton wool. Most insulating materials rely on trapped air to stop heat flowing away.

Keeping warm

Find out which insulating material keeps a hot drink hottest for the longest.

You will need:
- Four china mugs
- A polythene bag with tie handles
- Four thin rubber bands
- Newspaper
- Cotton wool
- Hand-hot water
- A clock

1 Wrap newspaper around a mug and secure it with a rubber band. Cover mug 2 with cotton wool. Place mug 3 upright in an open polythene bag and leave mug 4 uncovered.

2 Ask an adult to heat water until it is hand-hot (45°C). Fill each mug to the same level, 2cm from the top. Seal the polythene bag with a rubber band so it fits loosely around the mug.

Testing heat conduction

Stick a bead to the handle end of each spoon with a blob of butter. Stand the bowl on the newspaper and arrange the spoons in the bowl, handles outward. Ask an adult to pour boiled water into the bowl. Time how long it takes for the bead to drop from each spoon.

You will need:

- Butter
- Newspaper
- A heat-proof glass bowl
- Three small plastic beads
- Boiled water (ask an adult)
- Metal, plastic and wooden spoons

What's going on?

Conduction carries heat up the handle of each spoon, until the butter melts and the bead falls off. Of the three, metal is the best conductor. The metal spoon becomes hot quickest so the bead drops off this spoon first. The bead falls last from the wooden spoon because wood contains air and is a poor conductor of heat.

3 After 15 minutes, use a finger to test the water in each mug. Arrange the four mugs in order, from the hottest down to the coolest.

Solids, liquids and gases

Our world is made from millions of different materials, but all this matter exists in just three main forms – as solid, liquid or gas. Solids, such as ice cubes, are hard and have a fixed shape. Liquids, such as water, are runny, have no fixed shape, have a flat surface and fill the bottom of a container. Gases spread out in all directions, so they are often kept in a closed container.

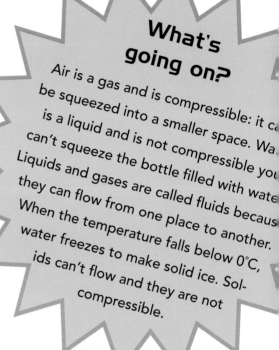

What's going on?

Air is a gas and is compressible: it ca be squeezed into a smaller space. Wa is a liquid and is not compressible you can't squeeze the bottle filled with wate Liquids and gases are called fluids becaus they can flow from one place to another. When the temperature falls below 0°C, water freezes to make solid ice. Solids can't flow and they are not compressible.

Feel the difference

See what happens when you try to squeeze a gas (air), a liquid (water) and a solid (ice). Take extra time to make the ice in step 3!

You will need:

- An empty 500ml bottle with a screw cap
- Water
- A long balloon
- A freezer

1 Take the empty bottle, with its cap screwed on tightly, and squeeze it in your hand. What happens to the bottle?

2 Now unscrew the cap and fill the bottle with water until it overflows. Screw the cap on tightly and squeeze the bottle again. Is it still squashy?

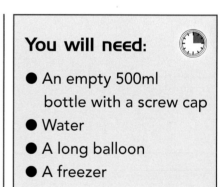

3 Fill a balloon with water (over a sink!) and tie it tightly. Squeeze the balloon and feel how the water moves around inside it. Place the balloon in a freezer for one hour. Now see if you can move the water around inside the balloon.

Gases have mass

Tie a piece of string to each end of the wooden rod. Tie the other ends of the string to the ring-pull on the cans. Hang the rod by its centre from underneath the stool so that the cans are balanced. Ask an adult to open one can slightly, then let the cans hang in balance.

What's going on?

The balance of the cans is disturbed and the open can rises slightly. This is because fizzy drinks contain a gas called carbon dioxide dissolved in flavoured water. When the can is opened, the carbon dioxide escapes slowly from the liquid, causing the mass of the liquid to decrease. This means the contents of the open can weigh less than they did when it was closed.

You will need:

- Two cans of fizzy drink with ring-pulls
- A thin wooden rod, 30cm long
- A kitchen stool or chair
- String

13

Mixing materials

Most materials are not one single, pure substance. They are usually made up of different substances mixed together in different ways. For example, pastry dough is a mixture of flour, fat and water, while fizzy drinks consist of water, sugar, flavourings and carbon dioxide gas. The right ingredients must be chosen to make up each different mixture.

What's going on?

Sugar and salt crystals dissolve (break down) when they are mixed with water. We call the result a sugar (or salt) solution. When the crystals dissolve, they break into particles too small to see. These particles spread through the water. Dissolved substances freeze at a lower temperature than pure liquids, so the sugar and salt solutions take longer to freeze than the pure water. Unlike sugar and salt, sand is 'insoluble' – it doesn't dissolve.

Solutions

We can mix water with sugar or salt to make something called a solution. The solution behaves differently to ordinary water.

You will need:

- Warm water
- Solid materials such as sugar, salt and sand
- Four clear plastic cups
- A teaspoon
- A magnifying glass
- A freezer

I Place a few grains of each solid on the table. Look at them through the magnifying glass. Can you see a difference in their shape and size? The grains of salt and sugar have straight sides – they are called crystals.

2 Half fill one of the cups with warm water. Add a pinch of sugar and watch what happens to each grain. Then add a heaped spoonful of sugar and stir the mixture. Notice how the grains dissolve and then disappear completely.

Investigating cake mixture

Ask an adult to help you collect all the ingredients and equipment needed to bake some small cakes. Watch how the ingredients change as you mix them together. See the mixture change again after it is baked in the oven.

You will need:

- Ingredients and kitchen equipment for baking cakes
- An oven

3 Half fill another cup with water. Place this, and the cup of sugary water, in the freezer for two or three hours. Try to look at them every 15 minutes to see what's happening. Now repeat steps 2 and 3 with the salt, and then with the sand.

What's going on?

It's amazing how different a baked cake looks and tastes from the original raw ingredients. Cake mixture usually contains flour, eggs, sugar and fat. While it cooks in the oven, heat makes the mixture expand, and changes its colour, texture and taste.

15

Expansion and contraction

When solids, liquids and gases are heated, they take in energy and their temperatures rise. As this happens, each substance expands: its volume increases and it takes up more space. As the substance cools, it loses energy. Its temperature and volume decrease and the substance contracts, or gets smaller.

What's going on?

The warm cloth heats the bottle and the air inside it. Heat energy makes the tiny particles of air move around faster and take up more space. As a result, the air expands and bubbles out of the straw. Cooling the bottle has the opposite effect. The particles slow down and take up less space. The air contracts, and water enters the bottle.

Hot and cold air

This activity helps you to see how air – an invisible gas – expands and contracts when it is heated and cooled. Ask an adult to help you with the glass and the hot water.

You will need:

- An empty glass bottle
- A drinking straw
- Modelling clay
- A dish cloth
- Hot water (ask an adult)
- A cold, wet cloth
- A bowl of water

1 Gently wrap a ball of modelling clay around the straw near to one end. Push the clay firmly into the neck of the bottle to make an airtight seal.

2 Ask an adult to soak the dish cloth in hot water and wrap it around the bottle.

3 Turn the wrapped bottle upside down and dip the end of the straw under the water in the bowl. What do you notice?

Heating water

Use the same equipment as before, but fill the bottle to the top with cold water before you fit the straw. Make sure some water rises about halfway up the straw, and mark its position. Now stand the bottle in a bowl of hot water and watch the water level in the straw.

You will need:

- A bottle, modelling clay and a straw, as before
- A bowl of hot water (ask an adult)
- A pencil

What's going on?

The particles in water move more slowly than the particles in air. Liquid particles are closer together than gas particles and must slide past each other as they move. Heating water makes the particles move faster, which makes the liquid expand and rise up the straw. But the effect is not so great as the expansion of gases.

4 Keep the end of the straw under the water's surface. Unwrap the hot cloth, then wrap the cold cloth around the bottle. Now what happens to the water?

17

Heating substances

When you heat a substance, its temperature rises. This rise causes many substances to change. For example, boiling water bubbles and bread becomes toast. When heating stops, the temperature falls. Water stops bubbling, so the change is only temporary, but cooled toast does not become bread again. Heat has caused a permanent change.

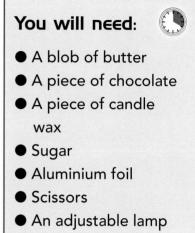

You will need:

- A blob of butter
- A piece of chocolate
- A piece of candle wax
- Sugar
- Aluminium foil
- Scissors
- An adjustable lamp
- A drinking straw

Gentle heating

Some substances change when the temperature rises only slightly. When you do this activity, don't touch the bulb – it will get hot.

I Cut out four 10cm squares of aluminium foil. Fold up the edges and pinch the corners to make four small boxes with an open top and a flat bottom.

2 Put a small amount of each substance into the aluminium boxes so that each box contains something different.

3 Ask an adult to switch on the lamp and point it straight down, about 5cm above the boxes. Wait five minutes to see what the heat does.

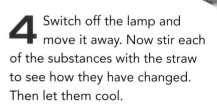

4 Switch off the lamp and move it away. Now stir each of the substances with the straw to see how they have changed. Then let them cool.

High-temperature heating

Place some sugar on an old teaspoon. Ask an adult to light the nightlight and hold the spoon over it for a while to heat it. What do you see?

What's going on?

Sugar is made up from carbon, hydrogen and oxygen. When heated to about 500°C, it breaks down into black carbon and steam, which is what you see beginning to happen on the spoon. When this happens, we say the sugar decomposes. It is a permanent change.

You will need:

- An old teaspoon
- Sugar
- Matches (ask an adult)
- A nightlight in a saucer of water

What's going on?

The lamp raises the temperature to about 75°C and gently heats the four substances. Remember that water boils when we heat it to 100°C. The butter, chocolate and candle wax all become liquids when they are gently heated, because they have melted. When they cool down, they become solids again so melting is a temporary change. Sugar is not affected by the heat from an electric lamp and so does not change at all.

High-temperature heating
ASK AN ADULT TO DO THIS FOR YOU.

Changing state

Matter can exist in three states – as solids, liquids or gases. When we heat a substance, it sometimes changes its state. Heat can make a solid melt to form a liquid, or a liquid boil to form a gas. These changes of state are temporary because cooling reverses them. Gases condense into liquids, and liquids freeze and become solid again.

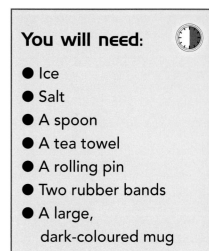

You will need:

- Ice
- Salt
- A spoon
- A tea towel
- A rolling pin
- Two rubber bands
- A large, dark-coloured mug

Gas to liquid to solid

The air is full of invisible water vapour. You can use a freezing mixture to trap this gas and turn it into ice, which you can see.

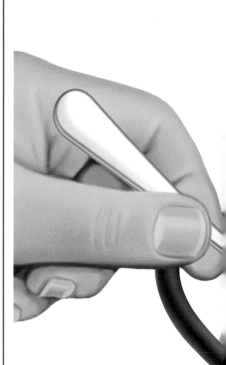

1 Place ten ice cubes along one edge of the tea towel and roll it into a sausage shape. Twist a rubber band around each end of the tea towel and place it on a firm surface. Now crush the ice with the rolling pin.

2 Half fill the mug with the crushed ice. Add about a quarter of a mugful of salt. Stir the mixture and then leave the mug undisturbed for about 20 minutes.

3 You will see that a white solid forms on the outside of the mug. It reaches up to the same level on the outside as the ice and salt inside. Scrape some of the solid into the spoon and watch it melt to form a liquid.

What's going on?

The temperature of ice drops even lower when salt is added. The mixture inside the mug makes the outside extremely cold. Air is a gas that contains water vapour dissolved in it. When this invisible vapour touches the outside of the mug, it condenses – which means it changes into liquid water. This immediately freezes into solid ice. When you scrape some of this into the spoon, it warms up and melts to form liquid water.

Boiling and evaporation

Wet two cotton handkerchiefs and wring them out. Hang one in a warm or sunny place and the other in a cool place. Check every five minutes to see how each hanky is drying.

You will need:

- Two cotton handkerchiefs
- A warm spot indoors
- A cool place
- Water

What's going on?

The wet hanky in the warm place dries faster than the one in the cool place. But why? As water takes in heat from the surrounding air, it changes and becomes a gas called water vapour. We say that the water has evaporated and the higher the temperature, the quicker the rate of evaporation. So, the hanky in the warm place dries faster than the one in the cool place because the water evaporates from it more quickly.

21

Filtering mixtures

Muddy water is an example of a suspension. It consists of tiny solid particles scattered through a liquid. To separate the particles from the suspension, you can use a filter. Filters work like sieves, but they have microscopic holes called pores, and are often made from thick, fluffy paper. The liquid part of a suspension passes through the holes between the paper fibres, while the solid particles are trapped.

You will need:

- A coffee filter funnel
- Coffee filter paper
- Water
- Plain flour
- Three clear plastic tumblers
- A teaspoon

Filtering flour

Mixing flour with water makes a cloudy suspension. Coffee filter paper makes the water clear again.

1 Add half a teaspoon of flour to a tumbler. Fill it with water and stir to make a suspension of flour in water.

2 Place the funnel in an empty tumbler and put in a filter paper. Pour two-thirds of the mixture into the filter.

3 When the tumbler is about a third full, move the funnel and the filter on to the last tumbler.

22

What's going on?

At first, liquid runs quickly through the filter. Most solid particles are trapped, but some small particles pass through. As a result, the filtered liquid in the first tumbler is slightly hazy. Liquid then passes slowly as the filter pores get blocked. Now even very small particles cannot pass, so the filtered liquid in the third tumbler is almost clear.

Filtering through sand

Cut the bottle in half. Place the funnelled end face down into the base of the bottle. Fill the bottle with cotton wool, pebbles, gravel and sand to make your filter. Then pour in mixed compost and water. Does it drip through fast? What colour are the drips?

You will need:

- A 500ml plastic drinks bottle
- Potting compost
- Sand, gravel, pebbles
- Cotton wool
- Scissors
- Water

What's going on?

The pebbles, gravel and sand – and the fibres in the cotton wool – act as a filter. They prevent the solids in the water from passing through. The trapped solids are called the residue and the liquid that passes through is the filtrate. Our tap water often comes from rivers and lakes. Huge sand filters make the water clear and pure. Added chemicals kill germs.

4 Look inside the filter paper when all the liquid has run through. Now look at the difference between the liquids in each tumbler.

23

Solutions and suspensions

Substances such as salt and sugar dissolve in water – they are soluble. When mixed with water, soluble substances disappear as they dissolve to form a solution. Substances such as chalk and sand do not dissolve in water – they are insoluble. Shaking an insoluble substance in water scatters their particles and forms a mixture called a suspension.

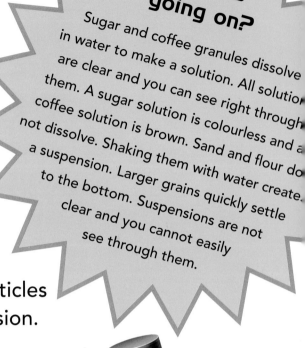

What's going on?

Sugar and coffee granules dissolve in water to make a solution. All solutions are clear and you can see right through them. A sugar solution is colourless and a coffee solution is brown. Sand and flour do not dissolve. Shaking them with water creates a suspension. Larger grains quickly settle to the bottom. Suspensions are not clear and you cannot easily see through them.

Solution or suspension?

Add different solids to water and decide which dissolve to form a solution and which scatter to make a suspension.

You will need:

- Four 500ml plastic bottles with caps
- Water
- A teaspoon
- A plastic funnel
- Sugar, fine sand, instant coffee granules, plain flour

1 Put one spoonful of sugar into a bottle. Use the plastic funnel to guide the crystals in. Add the sugar slowly so that it does not block the neck of the funnel.

2 Repeat step 1, placing each of the other solids in its own bottle. Half fill each bottle with water and screw on the cap. Shake each bottle ten times.

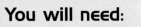

Investigating milk

Is milk a solution or a suspension? Find out by adding just one or two drops of milk to a glass of water. Look closely as the milk falls through the water.

You will need:

- A tall, clear plastic tumbler of water
- Milk
- A teaspoon

3 Look carefully at each bottle to see if you can still see solid particles. Decide which solids form a solution and which form a suspension.

What's going on?

You cannot see clearly through milk, even when you add it to water. Milk consists of droplets of fat suspended in water. Fat is insoluble in water and the droplets are too small for them to settle. Scientists call mixtures like milk 'emulsions'. This name is also given to emulsion paint, which consists of microscopic coloured droplets of oil suspended in water.

Evaporating solutions

You can make a solution by dissolving a solid such as salt in water. This looks like pure water because the solid has broken down into tiny invisible particles. To make the solid reappear, you can make the solution evaporate, or turn into a gas. As the liquid disappears, the solid reappears.

You will need:

- Salt
- Warm water
- A saucer
- A clear plastic tumbler
- A teaspoon

Evaporating salt solution

Solid salt seems to disappear when it dissolves in water. You can evaporate the water to get the solid salt back again.

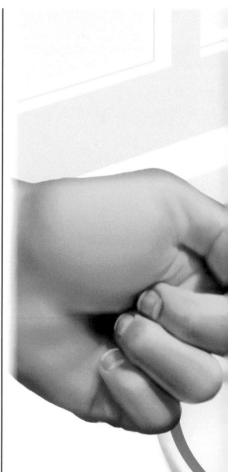

1 Pour warm water into the tumbler until it is one-third full. Add a spoonful of salt and stir the mixture until all the salt has dissolved.

2 Pour the salt solution into the saucer until there is a shallow pool, then put the saucer on a sunny windowsill or in some other warm, airy place.

3 Check the saucer twice a day for the next two or three days. What do you notice appearing on the saucer as the water gradually disappears?

Stalactite on a string

You will need:

- A length of wool
- Two paper clips
- Hand-hot water
- A dish
- A spoon
- Two jars
- Sugar

Fill each jar three-quarters full with hot water, then stir in sugar until no more dissolves. Fix a paper clip to each end of the wool. Drop each end into a jar so the wool hangs down between the jars. Place a saucer between the jars and leave them in a warm place. Inspect the wool every day for about a week.

What's going on?

The solution in each jar is saturated – it is as full as it can be of dissolved sugar. The liquid soaks along the wool and collects at the lowest point between the jars. Water evaporates here, so the solid cannot remain dissolved. Sugar crystals form and grow, as the wool soaks up more solution from the jars.

What's going on?

Heat causes the water to evaporate – it changes into an invisible gas called water vapour, which escapes into the air. As the liquid slowly evaporates from the solution into the air, the dissolved salt stays behind. You will see a crusty layer of solid salt left behind on the saucer once all the water has evaporated.

Saturated solutions

How much sugar can you dissolve in a cup of coffee? The answer is about 20 spoonfuls. If you add any more, solid sugar stays undissolved at the bottom of the cup. When a solution cannot dissolve any more solid, it is called a saturated solution. The amount of solid needed to make a saturated solution varies from one substance to another.

What's going on?

Each tumbler contains the same amount of water to make sure the test is fair. More sugar dissolves than salt, so sugar is more soluble than salt. Less bicarbonate of soda dissolves than sugar or salt, so it is the least soluble of the substances.

How much solid?

The solubility of a substance is the amount needed to make a saturated solution. Different substances have different solubilities.

You will need:

- Bicarbonate of soda
- Salt
- Sugar
- Six teaspoons
- Three clear plastic cups
- Water
- Sticky labels and pen

Soda

1 Label each of the tumblers 'sugar', 'salt', etc. Half fill them with water and place a teaspoon in each.

2 Add a teaspoon of sugar to the 'sugar' tumbler. Stir until it has dissolved. Repeat this step in the other tumblers using bicarbonate of soda and salt.

3 Add more solid to each tumbler until no more will dissolve. Count how many spoonfuls of solid dissolve in each tumbler.

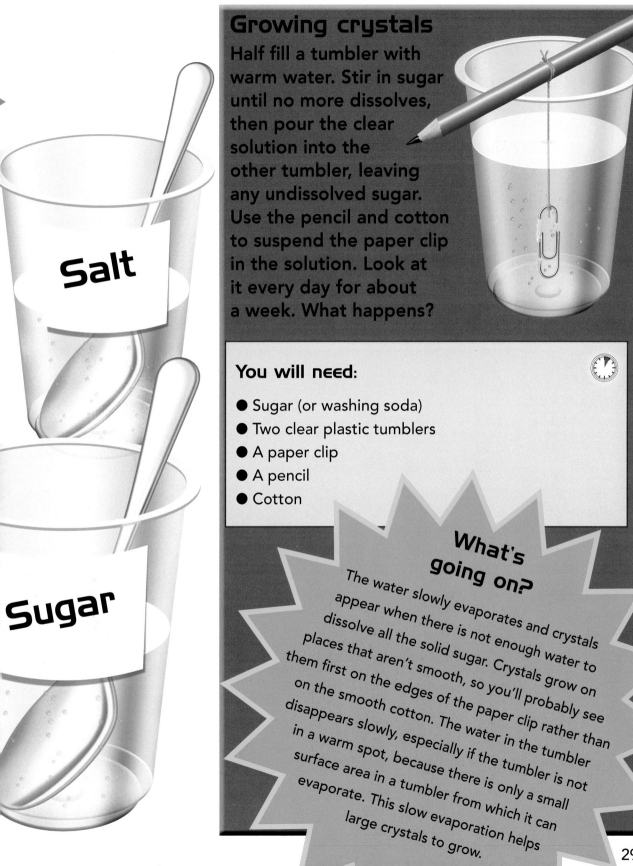

Growing crystals

Half fill a tumbler with warm water. Stir in sugar until no more dissolves, then pour the clear solution into the other tumbler, leaving any undissolved sugar. Use the pencil and cotton to suspend the paper clip in the solution. Look at it every day for about a week. What happens?

You will need:

- Sugar (or washing soda)
- Two clear plastic tumblers
- A paper clip
- A pencil
- Cotton

What's going on?

The water slowly evaporates and crystals appear when there is not enough water to dissolve all the solid sugar. Crystals grow on places that aren't smooth, so you'll probably see them first on the edges of the paper clip rather than on the smooth cotton. The water in the tumbler disappears slowly, especially if the tumbler is not in a warm spot, because there is only a small surface area in a tumbler from which it can evaporate. This slow evaporation helps large crystals to grow.

Salt

Sugar

29

Glossary

BOIL When a liquid is heated and reaches boiling point, bubbles form, rise to the surface and burst, releasing vapour. Boiling is the fastest form of evaporation.

CHEMICAL A single, pure substance. Salt is a chemical that chemists call sodium chloride.

CHEMIST A scientist who studies how permanent changes can make new substances. Remember that the people in charge of chemists' shops are called pharmacists. They prescribe medicines.

COMPRESS To squeeze something so that its volume decreases and it takes up less room than before. It is fairly easy to compress gases. It is almost impossible to compress liquids or solids.

CONDENSE To change a gas into a liquid, usually by cooling it.

CONDUCTOR A solid that allows heat (and electricity) to pass easily through it. Metals such as copper and aluminium are good conductors.

CONTRACT When an object becomes smaller. Most solids, and all liquids and gases, contract when they cool and their temperatures decrease.

DISSOLVE When a substance disappears as it is mixed into a liquid. Salt dissolves in water to make a salt solution.

ELASTIC A solid that changes shape when squeezed or stretched, then returns to its original shape when the squeezing or stretching stops.

ENERGY Energy is needed to make things happen. It is the ability to do work. Heat and electricity are two types of energy. Fuels contain energy that is released as heat when they burn.

EVAPORATE When a liquid changes into a vapour (gas), usually by heating it.

EXPAND When an object becomes larger. Solids, liquids or gases expand when they are heated and their temperatures increase.

FILTRATE The liquid part of a suspension that passes through a filter.

FORCE A push or a pull. Force can do work and make things speed up, slow down, or change shape. Forces can also cancel each other out when they push or pull against each other.

FREEZE When a liquid changes into a solid, usually through cooling.

HEAT A form of energy. When heat flows into an object, its temperature increases. Temperature decreases when heat flows out of an object.

INSOLUBLE Describes a substance that does not dissolve in liquid.

INSULATOR A substance that does not easily allow heat – or electricity – to pass through it.

LENGTH A measurement of the distance between two places. A unit of length is the metre (m). One metre equals 100 centimetres (cm) or 1,000 millimetres (mm). One kilometre (km) is equal to 1,000m.

MASS The amount of matter in an object. The unit of mass is the kilogram (kg).

MATERIAL Different kinds of solids. Steel, paper, skin, stone and plastic are all materials.

MATTER Anything that has mass and takes up space.

MELT When a solid changes into a liquid, usually through heating.

PERMANENT Describes a change that cannot easily be reversed.

PRESSURE A measurement of the amount of force pressing on the surface of an object. Your feet exert pressure on the floor. The pressure of the air inside a balloon keeps the skin stretched outwards.

RAW MATERIALS Natural substances that are used to make useful products. Raw materials are extracted from the ground (e.g. iron ore, crude oil), from seawater (e.g. bromine and iodine for use in medicines) and from the air (e.g. oxygen and nitrogen).

SATURATED SOLUTION
A solution in which no more solid can dissolve.

SOLIDIFY When a liquid changes into a solid, usually through cooling.

SOLUBILITY A measurement of how much solid or gas dissolves in a fixed amount of liquid.

SOLUBLE Describes a substance that will dissolve in a liquid.

SOLUTION The mixture that results when a substance dissolves in a liquid.

SUBSTANCE Any kind of matter. A substance can be a solid, a liquid or a gas.

SUSPENSION A mixture made by shaking small, insoluble particles with a liquid.

TEMPERATURE Describes how hot or cold something is. On the Celsius temperature scale, water freezes at 0°C and boils at 100°C.

TEMPORARY Describes a change that can easily be reversed.

VAPOUR Another word for gas.

VOLUME An amount of space taken up by an object. A unit of volume is the litre (l).

WEIGHT The force on an object that results when gravity pulls on its mass. Gravity on Earth is six times stronger than on the Moon, so objects weigh more on Earth.

Websites

If you have enjoyed this book, the websites below will give you even more information on matter and materials. Many of them have fun games to play that will help you to understand the difficult bits.

Matter:
- www.woodlands-junior.kent.sch.uk/revision/
  Science/changingmaterials.htm
- www.chem4kids.com/files/matter_intro.html
- www.wartgames.com/themes/science/matter.html

Materials:
- www.bbc.co.uk/schools/ks2bitesize/science/materials/
- www.museumnetworkuk.org/materials/index.html
- www.bgfl.org/bgfl/custom/resources_ftp/
  client_ftp/ks3/science/changing_matter/index.htm

31

Index